Dirt and All Its Dense Labor

Dirt and All Its Dense Labor

Poems by Gabriel Welsch

WordTech Editions

Published by WordTech Editions
P.O. Box 541106
Cincinnati, OH 45254-1106

Typeset in Baskerville by WordTech Communications LLC,
Cincinnati, OH

ISBN: 1933456329
LCCN: 2006904736

Poetry Editor: Kevin Walzer
Business Editor: Lori Jareo

Cover design: Jason Oakman
Cover photography: Jill Welsch

Visit us on the web at www.wordtechweb.com

Acknowledgments

Magazines in which the poems first appeared:

Crab Orchard Review: "Pennsylvania"
Harvard Review: "The Expensive View"
Chautauqua Literary Journal: "Pressing Business," "A Natural
    Selection"
Sou'wester: "Watershed"
Pennsylvania English: "Death and *Taxus,*" "The Oldest General
    Store in the State," "A Plantsman's Confession," "Worm
    Food," "*Cornus florida*"
Pinyon: "Land of the Car Radio"
Spoon River Poetry Review: "How We Are Made," "Ghost"
Baybury Review: "Pause"
Mid-American Review: "Considering Linnaeus," "Inoculation
    Time," "Wave-Particle Theory Approaching Mid-October,"
    "Full Moon, January Thaw"
5AM: "A Gardener's Prayer"
Inkwell: "Beer Bottle," "The Rift," "Starting Seeds"
Connecticut Poetry Review: "Talking To God"
Birmingham Poetry Review: "Vernal Equinox," "Killing Bees"
Marlboro Review: "Penance, West Virginia"
Lucid Stone: "Preserves"
The MacGuffin: "Two Hour Delay"
Many Mountains Moving: "Charlie in His 101st Year"
Beauty for Ashes Poetry Review: "Linnaeus Never Said a Peony Was
    Bashful"
Fourteen Hills: "Quartet on Beauty and Mystery"
From the Fishouse: A Digital Archive of Emerging Poets: "Night
    Thoughts in Central Pennsylvania" and "Birthplace of
    Memorial Day"

"Pennsylvania" is included in Marjorie Maddox and Jerry
Wemple's (ed.) *Common Wealth: Contemporary Poets on Pennsylvania*,
Penn State Press, 2005.

"Preserves" is included in David Garrison and Terry Hermsen's (ed.) *O! Taste and See: Food Poems*, Bottom Dog Press, 2004.

I extend great thanks to the editors and readers of the publications that first ran these poems. I also express gratitude to Robin Becker for her support, mentoring, friendship, and ever-careful eye. Particular thanks is reserved for other individuals whose supportive reading and criticism of the poems made them vastly better, including Dave Bonta, Camille-Yvette Welsch, and J. David Stevens. Special thanks also to Karen Craigo, Mike Czyzniejewski, Linda Dove, and the board of the Toledo Botanical Garden, for awarding me the Thoreau Artist-in-Residence at the Toledo Botanical Garden in September 2002, a period wherein many of the poems in this book either originated or underwent significant revision. Thanks to Matt O'Donnell, at *From the Fishouse*, (www.fishousepoems.org) where digital recordings of my reading some of the poems in the book can be heard. Thanks also to the Pennsylvania Council on the Arts for a literature fellowship in 2003. Saint's Coffeehouse and the crowd of supporters there made for a wonderful place in which to begin many of these poems. Finally, heartfelt gratitude to my family for their years of support, with the greatest thanks going to my wife, Jill.

For Jill Renee and Isabella Yvette

Contents

I. Our Earthly Trust

Pennsylvania

after Bishop

The state with the prettiest name
and the ear of an ancient ridge—
its runnel of stone cluttered
with the wet trees that hold taut
the devastating brown in winter,
the state with air cluttered by the noise
of more miles of road
than any other state, its cities
rarefied by steel and freedom—
the state of deer hungry and baffled,
twisted on its roads, tufted on its fenders,
swinging husks on the porches
of tight homes crowded on the Susquehanna,
the Juniata, the Allegheny—
the state where roads of chicory
rattle through the weight of August
out of the mountains and onto the slow
limestone slab that runs to the Chesapeake—
the state hollowed out in its wood-dense
middle, rusted in a line from Scranton
to Monroeville, slag heaps stand sentry
over ridges pillaged bald—
the state on fire at its core where stories
slide into the maw of hell each time
another house groans its way into the earth—
the state abutting the Great Lakes
which feels their force with each gush
of winter that rakes over the ridges—
the state where mud sings, its telepathy
gritty and familiar, its voice a particular
shade of its character, given roundness
with sweet lime—
the state of forests that beckon
with trails of shadow and distance and great

disappearance, tied to its deliberate
stretch toward winter, when this state is all smoke
and the gray reaches of trees, all darkness
and fire, all ash and water and the salt-worn
roads that lead all thoughts to home—
the state where to talk of soup is to talk
of God and Sunday bundling and bazaars
through the countryside and gravestones
laid over with flags and wax begonias—
the state with pierogie sales and funnel cakes
and cheesesteaks and soft pretzels
and the ruddy faces of corpulent railroaders—
the state that is everywhere and here,
made distinct by its bunched mountains
and hidden towns, how it lays demolished
under leaves, resting on ground that grows
hollow and more hollow year after year,
burning and sinking—
the state with the prettiest name, a name
that is both lie and promise,
adjective and mystery, history and fable,
one man's woods.
We hear robins in the laurel, semis
jake-braking into town,
the sudden snap of deer hooves
on tomato stakes. And always,
highways building and seething
with our weight, pushing on limestone,
building and building on this softening ground.

The Expensive View

—title taken from a line by D. Nurkse

He spoke about his wife in pursed euphemism—
"We decided to raise our children with one
parent always at home."
From his suit—chalked and smooth at once—
to his shoes, soft calf bellies like a gilding
for the foot, I expected a tumbler of whisky
in Manhattan's throb of afternoon—
a clear tumbler, to see the amber
bought with lavish time and oak—
but he drank water, from a thin tap
behind his uncluttered desk. I was there
to write a fawning story of what he'd earned
to a less affluent readership, but the expensive view
kept drawing me to its jumbled progression
of stacked deeds pointing to the sea.
Of course he drank water! Afternoon drinkers,
the reprobate among us, earn indulgence but rarely
an aerie for surveying those who would undo them.
The expensive view, so much real estate, so much cost
of all that is buried under this leafless jungle,
and this man in the bunker of his euphemisms—
"I've done what it takes," he says. "It's like the song:
if you can make it here, you can make it anywhere."
I wrote later that his hair swept back like a Renaissance
poet's, let him chuckle at his own wit, his depiction
of himself as a bygone dilettante. I want to say
I felt the cheap sting of my own smugness, knowing
the card house of my own euphemisms stood tall
as well. I thought him rich, pompous, a stretch
of his own skin and wit. I couldn't look at him,
except to find details: platinum lapel pin, jade cufflinks,
chin cleft, mole behind the ear. The tape ran

while I took in the view, a sky as clear as his forehead,
not a cloud or a plane or even a reflection of light
off the ocean that, from here, looked so small.

Pressing Business

Trees leaf out—roses and lilacs
sequin with buds. Smooth tense skins
tighten like a promise. We'll break them down.
We'll press them, force them flat
for a record. Press them within the pages
of an unabridged dictionary, the RHS
encyclopedia of gardening. Let them feel
the weight of the language we have heaped
upon them. The weight is heavy indeed:
philosophy, the bible, a dictionary,
a Rookwood pot—terra cotta, urn-shaped,
paperbacks stuffed inside, the weight
of more learning and cultural import
to crush the color of a tulip flat, a tulip
that had come a long time down to this,
pushed in a towel in a dictionary under a pot,
this blossom of Dutch monarchs, this Mercedes
of mercantilism, this blossom to kill a king for, this
delicate gem of no facets. We write the tags,
take their names and learn them,
speak them in our home, teach their curves
to our tongue and teeth, feel
language work even here, simply by its
accumulated weight. In this way,
syllables blossom, the names lose
their context of weeds, keep the color
slipped from the sun.

A Natural Selection

"Nature does not proceed by leaps." —Linnaeus

Here and there
the minute stutter of biology
works from quill to spur,
vesicle to panicle to lisp,
building the traits that mean
we adapt. The pitch pine coats its cones
in resin so it only sprouts in the fires
that savage every century or so;
the dromedary hump defines
the depth of deserts. Given that lexicon
what of the far less delicate
bomb, the maladaptive urge to resign,
or the simple singleness of murder?
If I can make it past this question
and its jumble of mutations—
well, who's to say? There float yet more
mysteries—the fragile bow
of the ulna, the specifics required
by seeds, the varying sizes
of lenticels, all those floss thin
signs of circumstance,
fronds tested time and again
by the unseen wonder of wind.

—for David J. Welsch

Watershed

"—the little we get for free,
the little of our earthly trust. Not much."
            —Eizabeth Bishop, "Poem."

Wine bottles in recycle bins all down the block
glint the last light of a dry June evening,
a Sunday, make deep shadows in the new grass,
a peony a splayed burst

of another light glowing in Northern rooms
as the cool descends with maple seeds
and the street rests, yards quiet and dense
with grill heat and early honeysuckle

lining the stream at the hill's bottom. The stream
runs southeast, behind an auto body shop, a printer,
out beneath a laureled ridge and on past Dublin
and Rising Sun, to a confluence of streams

from Pennsylvania, Delaware, Maryland, into the slow
Chesapeake, its snails and curvaceous clams,
its silted bottom and illusory green, the true exotic,
so far from here—from the coiled hose,

the mailbox flag, the forsythia clutched in English ivy,
the tuft of clipped grass, the soapy husks of lather left
in the driveways where we washed cars—far, far from ease,
from these rooms now clasped in evening.

Death and Taxus

Yews are old; in graveyards they tent
over the dead, their berries blood heavy
blackening stones.

In our suburbs they crouch as battlements
in front of ranches and bungalows
whispering "Eisenhower."

Their botanical call is the drum beat
of perpetuity: *Taxus baccata baccata*
Taxus repandens—

the beat for the oarsman to stroke over Styx,
the stone in the prow, his face like the pit
of yew berries.

Taxus, taxus, take from us our light,
the tilth of our soil, our fears,
our house fronts, our sorrow. Make it green.

The Oldest General Store in the State

Each year, a journalist photographs the sign
for the last working bomb shelter in the county,
in the oldest general store in the state.
Every other year, a painter repaints it.
Behind the bomb shelter sign, other side of the wall,
grumped in old catalogs and out-of-date phone books,
the store owner gazes at tits on tool calendars,
a red circle foreseeing this day. Today
the painter comes to touch up the blue and gold.

All day scrapple goes quick from the meat case,
sap buckets clang by the hand-cranked registers
and mechanics buy Dickies from women
crowned in hair nets and flannel aprons.
Farmers linger by the long front windows,
grouse about traffic, construction, and Kerry—
they spit, brag football, and feel chummy
with George the fix-it man, whose bum leg,
half-eaten by diabetes, bumps the floors.

The owner's tie hangs limp on his bulk,
and the slugs of his lips part to ask
a girl for coffee. The painter's van rolls up,
and he strolls trailing a fog of his last smoke,
spattered pants pooled at his boots, tattoos turned to blue.
Once the painter is started, the owner's Caddie
will slink out the back parking lot. Later,
the owner will gasp and clutch his chest,
miss a red light and kill a mother.
He'll have left a long lunch with a plumbing
supplier, fermented breath and backed up
acid. Lumber men will shake their heads.
The butcher will drink in the cooler.

But this day the painter pours his tarp,
shakes a can, begins to paint, the cleft

of his ass flashing like a white light.
He tapes off the atomic triangles,
careful not to disturb this place
where stock sprouts dust, and clerks leave it
unwittingly preserved, well versed themselves
in the journalism of others' nostalgia. Their yawns
threaten like convicts, and cigarette packs hover
on the counters, by surly penny dishes,
beautiful curls of receipts.

Land of the Car Radio

I.
My brother, a lively bastard then,
bleary and bellicose, cursed most things—

school, work, his truck, money, women—
while we drove on weekends to work,

to dust and fences, dawn risings, days of heavy sun.
Route 322, beers between our legs,

empties clinking on the floor, windows open
shivering to Creedence and bayous and Buck Owens

willows arcing in their classic sorrow,
slapped by the tumble of wind from thousands of wheels

we spoke little, grumbles about hay bales,
cows, post-holes and gravel, the tractor's temper

and the road rumbled, ash below us
through rust spots in the floor.

II.
Along 322, poplars, maples clutching
to limestone river edges,

spring houses and satellite dishes
hunker equal in the landscape,

country sidled along at a varied step,
the counties' brooks singing under brick

bridges to houses near outlet pipes.
We drove so late some nights,

from school to farm, the radio whine

bit the stiff, white breeze

as we sipped beers, noted a woman's grace
washing dishes and spotting our truck.

I imagined stories for her, Big Wheels and crayons,
dishes crusty with potatoes, husband distracted

hands rough from a mill and distance is good
for me, as I like humanity as a whole—

its epics, its struggles—but squirm at details
of humans: bills, thimbles, waistbands and sweat

goldfish in jars, empty lighters, romance novels
and the need for well-lit stores.

I hope her eyes, flickering over us, are lined,
heavy without shade, bleary from contacts.

From the blue strobe of TV in windows
deep with implied furnishings,

elsewhere a child gaped at the road, his gaze
in a frozen frame, under a maple whose

roots reached down to constrict cables,
wires and pipes in mantle-deep

heritage deep as the rumble of highways bowing
under eighteen-wheelers stretching from clutch

to clutch of people wrapped in the same noise of babies,
car sales, church bells, backfires, steel guitars and static.

III.
Driving past Selinsgrove and Dauphin,
the road curved along the Susquehanna,

and when it was light enough we'd see

the leaning Statue of Liberty

in mid-river on flood-placed rocks.
Students built her out of blinds,

rowed out in heavy current
to her perch in the dark, where she

unbothered by pigeons and crows,
let her slatted features blur like water into

their small joke on freedom.
I often thought she peered across the river to

the shack bar "The Heidelberg"—
where even after boarded windows,

the parking lot a wave of weeds,
the sign still snagged headlights

and a tight, wood oval proclaimed "yes"
to those who passed—a fleet

of truckers and students and cops
and graveyard shifters and contractors and drifters,

a population as reduced and unlike the mythic
as the prank on freedom in the river.

IV.
Noise of stories, pink slips and maple syrup
straight from Maine and maples near Canada

and layoffs and the goddamned Japanese
and union cards, 30-packs of beer and love's lament

and well-digger rigs, run-off water and animal hooves
shuddering earth, barbed wire and construction zones

and all the same radio stations at rest in cars

lined up in constellated brake lights and glinting guard rails

and mutual fund commercials, diapers and high
whines and kitchen tables and decks of cards and poker

and empties and ticket stubs and the fine gray
detritus of lottery on the edge of a dime, chewing gum

and the lip smacks and garbled drive through and
grease guns, wrenches, tobacco and borrowed shovels

and picket fences and on, the stories evolving to song
to progressions to marketing to radio and commercials

and the link to people who have heard the same thing
so many times it is now the pristine clarity of static.

V.
And we talked, he and I, breath fogging windows
against the gray rain. We didn't know that soon

a woman would calm him with the smallest words,
and he would tell me I would be an uncle.

His speech is now rounded, softer syllables of praise
for his children, twins, a surprise and a burden

wound into a gift that quietly surprised him.
He hasn't married, and uncursed, an angel

of work and past sins, he is both unshaven and bleary,
and bending to kiss the twins' blond crowns,

a ghost of those highways and farms, the stories
that mortar the edges of my past and my mind,

and he rests at once as the edgy bastard who tossed coins
in a man's face, bus fare for a fired farmhand,

and the sudden father, his old truck packed high with bales
of diapers, folded stroller girders and a woman

in the front seat, who speaks to him with the muted
pleasure of familiarity, of time adjusted.

VI.
And, in the rooms crouched on the hills,
in the spotty, scrabble rock bent woods,

the ghosts of roadside windows watched
erosion's traffic, and buffeting winds

tear Liberty in the rush of semis.
Over the road noise, shrill through the air,

car radios—loud, intrusive, afloat—
scattered the air in tinny bursts,

tinnient blares shuddering
in the humid gel of stillness.

VII.
We stopped for gas, the hum in our ears
from road noise and lights, his eyes sunk

twitching from the dotted lines, we'd hear
the twang of steel guitar in stores,

from speakers over racks of old cassettes,
singing about work and love, and something

in that order, work and love, spoke to anyone
listening, connected by the wires and roads,

about the sweat and miles spent
to earn it; the music sings softness

in the voices, pain or pride, labor's dirty
wisdom or weariness of travel,

about how we're broken.
Our souls smaller from the effort, we're together,

squirreled in the foothill state, close with roads
and ears, wrapped in the same radio noise by

the static and silence and voices, town to town,
past farms and over highways to glittering settlements,

buffeted and softened, to our home in the noise.

How We Are Made

How the heart buffs its luster
and keeps to itself. How the face
denies its blood, pales against a breeze.

How the hands bend their bones
at the knuckles in late age. How the feet
flatten, spread, knuckle under at the toes.

How the eyes drift through clouds
and glints of heaven under lids,
to stars and linted clusters—dust.

How the elbows bunch with muscle,
how the skin thins to paper, how the waist
turns from anger, how the ears shine with wax.

How the mouth will slow and tremor, the teeth
knock the skull. How the lips will turn,
dry and crack, pull the flesh taut.

How the flesh will blister and rise,
cush and smooth. How we falter.
How we stroke ourselves to sleep.

2. Dirt and All Its Dense Labor

Epitaph

after Merwin

The winters I passed hours in ice light
hearing the melt through the roof
the sky in its milky cup
pressed star-distant
and I cradled days of quiet.

Springs I trod the green's insistence
tasting soil as though it weren't ancient
and simply repeated in new inflorescence
nearby as knees and damp
while I sowed what I remembered.

Summers I breathed in sheets of light
warmed with cricket screams and bees
leaves a shambling deep gloss
toothsome and handsome
and I bundled their scents to me to remember.

Autumns I hoped through leaf-spiced twilight
against the gilded glisten of limbs
cold firmament a cloud-thick distance
wind buoying the seeds on a breeze
to drop them to soil and a bedding of quiet.

Pause

after Frank O'Hara

If I am given a moment—
time plucked from a day—
I might wash in the thick cloth
of petunia fragrance, or iris musk,
mull over mud and let my tongue
empty through my teeth—loose
the words I would never say,
conversations fat and imagined
that clog my throat on purple days.
I'll stare at windows, guess
at the thickness of light
resting on the glass pushing out
from inside. Take the time inside
this poem and grow a fruit
of rest, let ideas marinate
in the spice of yew needles dying,
pressing at the breeze, their smell
on a cold night near limbed streets
insisting that the dark hides nothing
that doesn't want to be hidden.

To Isabella

April carries promises we know
each autumn will undo. Not this.
Stars will lend your birth meaning,
as will time, and so will we,
counting back to your conception,
to what must have been a July night
several moons before, grass fronds
old and blunted, primrose high
in the yard, the sky as endless
as all that lay ahead of us,
star-deep and shadowed by leaves.

I thought the world would change
in only one night,
fog crystallizing what moonlight stayed aloft
that early April, weed shadows
fringing the road—and it all looked
not yet imbued with difference—
just the newness that spring brings,
a green still fearing frost
and the yellow of so many
newly living leaves.

A Plantsman's Confession

"The plumber's sink is always clogged."
—folk proverb

Those squatters, swarthy green on my window sill,
wilt and twist, buckle at their pot rims.
With miserly watering, peace lily, pothos and devil's ivy
to subsist on neglect: dust, lined
like a dry river bed, mottles and cakes the leaves,
and the tendrils of peace lily slouch,
long withered, their veins dark and prominent in the aged tan,
like the whorled innards of a walnut.
What leaves remain on the umbrella tree spread undecided,
torn between sun at the window,
shadows of the side yard, veiled
solitude of the ceiling.

The spider mites weave boudoirs at the crotches
of stems and trunk. I see the pathogenic blight.
Though I can advise gardeners on tomatoes' real desires,
on lusher azaleas, on weed control, on exactly
what *gypsophila paniculata* has to do with limestone,
my window tells the true story of my work.
I toast the weeds in my unmulched beds, contradictions to all
my advice to garden customers. They
don't know I look forward to the drape
of sweetgrass, to the splay of a thistle bloom.

Worm Food

I let my syllables compost,
know the company of worms.

I want them rich with grub innards,
to take food from the gullet walls

of night crawlers. And if filled
with soil a night crawler

were broken in two underfoot,
let those ends burrow under roots,

evade moles, wiggle until it rains
and they resurface far from asphalt,

under the high-ribbed leaves of heaven,
to greet the mist as if it were new.

Inoculation Time

With new air and the old startle of sun,
the slopes return to green. Runnels
of water slice the brown hills of the pasture,
and the cattle sway across the slick rises,
toward the tufted green on the leeward end,
near where the trees hover like coal smoke.
Return to their breath, their matted haunches,
their air thick with the round heft of shit and hay,
the barn's tinnient echo of hoofs on concrete ramps,
the earthy smell of whitewash, the grit of lime.
Return to the calves, their stunning knotted legs,
their sure kicks and reeling eyes, their struggle
against you and the ropes. The first shot
promises the rest, the serene terror of those fields,
the rises thick with others, the road at the edge
a mystery of noise, and always, the tall shapes
among them with their hands, their curses.

Considering Linnaeus (1707-78)

Imagine a landscape unnamed,
    growth known only by legend and feel,
        as he must have seen it, fuzzy legend, mysterious
            lore,

Lady's Mantle named by the church, not for its hairy
    fan-palm leaves that offer pearls culled
        from morning's dew. He knew yarrow

would staunch the blood, that Achilles
    held fistfuls of leaves against the wounds of his men,
        the minted resin mixing with blood. He knew

these things, crabbed them down in Latin,
    imagined their names in more elegant syllables
        released from the tyranny of legend—

he gave to them precise identity.
    And his enemies, those men that scorned his Adamic
        notes and motions, those men too were
            immortalized,

their last names Latinated to become the botany
    of skunk cabbages, the spiny thistles, the lowest spurge,
        the tufts fought with sopping hoes and boiling water

that spawned industries of pollution and loathing.
    But the rest, beautiful and dear to him, grew
        more graceful, their names lush with iambs.

Mornings in the strangeness of fog, the unsettled dew,
    still heavy with sleep I crouch behind his eyes
        to navigate his landscape, a world of muddied tales,

to see landscape as a smear of legend, the ear not hearing names,
    just noticing the toothed edge of one leaf, or the eager

           stamens
    of a particular blossom, the frizz of seed heads
           browning as cell

walls fall down under the weight of coming sun and moist air.

A Gardener's Prayer

Ice glazes the spines of crocus leaves
a whorl of grass
like tufts of glass. Cold's chime
soothes this place—

where winter's last grip
of the long cold
afterward feels as though it went
quickly, a whisper

in a darkened train, while I rode
between stops unsure
I heard it until days later
it clattered through my dreams

toward morning with certainty.
I seldom need
reminding that I'll die—the sun
each day replays that truth.

The gritty nature of how
lives as a breath
worrying my ear. Amid crocus leaves
I dream a quiet end. May it be

as easy for me as a glaze of ice about
my leaves, a slick
of water to seal my eyes,
a cloud's weight to push me back to earth.

Beer Bottle

Even by the dry gold mornings of autumn we still
went to the daylily fields, coffee steamed and unshaven
to dig the roots, plunge our thumbs in the flesh,
pry the rhizomes apart, cup the fans into rows
for blossoms months away to flare and fade
in a single day. When the sun reached its height,
its blanket of light punched with chill wind,
we stood for the breeze, drank coffee
and ate soup from cartons, put new
cassettes in the tape deck. For me,
then, it was a job. I was so easily fooled.
I didn't know the full weight of propagation,
all the word held, the work itself a rhizome
able to twist its energies to whatever purpose
avails itself.

Labeling rows with Sharpies and plastic tags,
with metal sign placards and buried wire,
preserving the beds for another harvest of daylilies,
by the whitewashed barn we counted days
in numbers of fans, rows, divisions,
loss in busted rhizomes, fans too slender
to plant, that easy accounting a solid post
on which to hang a day. For years after I left,
I knew I could return to that barn, find
the Molson bottle stuffed in haste behind a spar
when you and I bleached the potting area
one February day. The boss arrived, and we stowed
our beers, hustled back to work. It provided
a home for spiders and worms, I suppose,
within that barn that I still smell in the leaf mold
breezes spinning pollen into a benediction.

—*for Tim Lang*

Talking to God

I will show you
lobelia shading a Malaysian pot
a mosquito afloat on rainwater
in a galvanized tub
sly flowers of lemon balm, their souls
given over to oil, to scent
malva's tumult of seed and bloom
an anemone speaking of an optimist's sky
sage reborn by a daisy's rotted leaves
coreopsis reaching for a meadow
wood poppy a lamp in the shade of a yew
a pot of basil to speak of love
its musky thick-leaved voice
dill among the peonies
thyme among the anise
the serenity of aconites
while I write this in the shade of iris leaves
where life is a shell, a pod of bloom yet to be
a confidence in roots, of the world as seen
over the smooth shoulder of petals
where a breeze is never more than wind.

Vernal Equinox

What happened that night with us? We bathed
Isabella, made a late dinner, graded papers
until past midnight, stepped carefully in the sounds
of the house which, like the ground, warmed
and opened, swelled its boards, creaked its pipes.
We had the rare contact with the lively
beginnings of iris, Lenten rose, and aconite
in our beds. What sentences return to us
each spring? How much of the heart
recalls its source in soil? The windows frame
the sky, our eye frames the world, a candle
frames the eye, the birch frames the air
about the house—is this so much stretching?

Linnaeus framed a mess of life in Latin's scaffold,
Bohr framed synaptic jumps and Rutherford
framed what we can neither see nor hold.
We listen and follow the herring-boned weave
of a concerto boxing our ears, stretching
and framing for us the evening's neat divide
of light, half day, half night, when spring
and birth collide, when a system
reveals itself in this cloven perfection
governing light.

If you search for it, the world can look
as though it boils down to two.
We checked on Isabella before bed,
looked into her crib. We know the soft
vulnerability of infants, know their sight
is all absorption. The light from outside
worked across her face, a veil of energy,
graded and stretched, not cloven but tattered
and ragged, dizzily uncertain, as it blended
to shadow and then to dark.

Penance, West Virginia

Hash marks in the back
cover of my catechism
made a careful record
of the count of sinful

lapses when I took
the Lord's name in vain.
In my mind, when the marks
reached the right number

my soul was doomed—each hash
a sliver that would in time
reconstruct a cross from my sins
to crucify Christ all over again.

Father Widowiac in his cloud
of sandalwood and garlic could smile
and endure my inventory
of small crimes: disobeying parents,

being mean to sister, even shoplifting—
but I never dared utter
what I had done to the name
of the father, never to the screen

that was priest and not priest,
that holy lurking terror that surely would
whisk over the votives and take
their light, that would cup

and stifle the censers, roll
on to the whitewater river
that threatened every year to rise
and wash us all away, and there

plunge me in for both baptism

and death, punishment and redemption,
my body a sudden stone
weighted with its weak curses.

Cornus florida

My grandmother says they crucified Christ
on a dogwood cross, and that's why
the trees' wood twists smaller now,
no longer stately, or board-feet straight.
Under a ceiling of taller trees' limbs,
the dogwoods blossom shell white, below
forest's leaves that trap the alchemy
of light, hold the day at bay, the smaller
trees in suspended dusk.

Smelling of loam and mint, she
told me the holy blood of Christ
scorched the painted blossom tips.
Each petal ends in a neat clip,
a fingernail curve where a drop of his blood
burned it clean. The blood rust
stains the petal's rib,
a last dull color, close to earth's hue,
before the blossom fades.

God bent the trees as retribution.
If they could walk—their trunk angles
swelled arthritic knobs, bark
straining at fattened crowns—they might
shuffle like her, shifting to move
each leg, accommodating her spine.
With bark flimsy as her skin, dogwoods now lack
the strength to crucify anyone, much less a god.

Rather, like hearth goddesses and miners,
like her back, the dogwoods—
bent forms in a forest's purgatory—
bear the world's canopy on feeble beauty.

—*for Vivian Wyant*

Ghost

This morning I vacuum my father's skin
off the hardwood floors of the back room.
The white flakes rub off as he dresses and undresses
at the ends of sleep, as it has shed for years,
the powder of him left in rooms and crevices,
rugs and the corners where arms meet a chair.
Psoriasis is the clinical name, a way of saying
there is too much of him, his skin grows too fast,
the body cannot hold it with his feeble gravity.
It is as if his body is too eager to return to earth. Part
of me hopes I will miss some of the skin, that a piece
will slip between the floorboards, that he will remain
with me long after the inevitable. Now he muses on his own
death. We can be driving to get apples or wood
and he will speculate on how well he will get to know
his grandchildren. He talks of the Civil War
soldiers he reads about, notes that even those
who survived wounds and disease were dead
by his age. He speaks more frankly about Viet Nam,
the boys who sunk dead into muddy land, and how now
he hears the creaks and bone whispers of his body.
I make myself remember we are not just our bodies,
but as the breeze drifts my father's skin
over the floor, I think of him
in the scales and the balm he rubs
into his arms and back, I think of the look
of his skin, the eruptions beginning on my own.
Such remnants can comprise ghosts, and ours
tell a story in dust—his sawdust and toast crumbs,
great cirrus clouds of plaster, the airborne soil
of a dry July, carbide dust, a coating of rust,
dust of iron on a whetstone. Mine is soil
from the dried roots of allium, pencil shavings
and wood ash, spring mud and winter salt.
All that we know tells us it is not as simple as
dust to dust. Dust gathers and floats,

settles on skins we keep so briefly,
before they swirl into storied soil,
a rebirth in dirt and all its dense labor.

3. Sharpened by Cold

Full Moon, January Thaw

Evenings like this promise false springs
as the moon waxes in its fog-sotted corona.
When the seasons mix, our time folds
forward on itself, that we might step
into memories unmade, early anniversaries,
earth-scented recollections. Bella, still
a stranger to the lushness of language,
may not yet know the days grow, instead
senses their length, remembers what she can
about time and weather, her instincts
perhaps less befuddled than our informed
ideas about time's arrangement with the seasons.
She might feel air more dense with light,
rich with predictions of rain, she might
feel in the ground's sigh a tuft of grass.
I wonder at her world, her sense at last.

Wave-Particle Theory Approaching Mid-October

If I sit here long enough can I learn
to understand light, how it occupies

the same air as sound, how dense
with us our air must be? Chopin notes,

pollen's ragged balls, the gas of conversation
and convection, the external air of internal combustion

engines, the fat, lively push of strobes
which never stop. Light has to go somewhere—

sparklers going without dissipation—
but how does friction work with light?

If light is a wave of energy, then resistance—bunched
electrons, botched connections, surly atoms

whose valences bramble light, absorb its energy,
exhaust it—or that clutter of radio, television,

cyberspace, reflected satellite chatter. If particles,
then dust, molecules of air, whole chains

of pollen and pheromones. Gilded, for sure,
in early autumn, light weighs little enough for air to carry it.

Its load, however minuscule, on leaves presses
their color to the surface, against dead

chloroplasts, like soap bubbles on glass,
the erratic veins of depth, of sun long ago

digested to green and down to red, with new
weight pressing at kin, at energy returned,

as the smell of passing leaves brings me faces
of cooler weather, evening strolls to beat

the darkness, the cold bite of my wedding day,
when the sky promised gold before the snow—

and which, each year, returns to make its promise:
stack wood soon, fuel to make it through.

Preserves

I cut back my shriveled garden this November,
all fruits gone, leaves frost crunched but fragrant
with the last stores of water rising to the snipped stems.
In other yards, scarfed gardeners bundle stakes,
cast neat squares with winter rye,
are soundless but for movement, harvest
long plucked like the mills and jobs
that built these homes. They snug potatoes
for winter, firm the mounds over onions,
while I cut back the odd ornament of roses,
lady's mantle, thyme and lavender.

Through these softened Appalachians,
western Pennsylvania towns crouch half hollow,
Main Street a straight shot to foundries and old rails
bleeding rust into the gravel, scrub dead
grass and bent underbrush by the turnpike.
People here wrinkle against the cold. They still
can, put up food, cure meat, hunt and hold church
bake sales, dances, festivals, card games. They
keep shelves of pillowy pears, firmed apple butter,
cabbage pressed to glass and tomatoes
glistening with stymied sun.

On these coldest days, snow is like dust,
twisting glass ghosting along salt routed
pavement and stretches of potholes.
The windows of downtown darken with emptiness
so deep I see the back walls of former stores.
Farm fences mimic hillocks at sight's edge,
where the sky is opaque milk crusted dry, and I see
only the slow steps of people in the fog,
grey as ghostly poplar trunks, hunched
shadows heavier than the cold's
pale or the wind-worn stone of storefronts.

On those days, I understand their pantry shelves,
and why my wife wicks summer into a Ball jar.
We want to smell the work of summer's
earth, our home when green and warm.
I crouched one day last August and pruned
the shrubby lavender stems pouched in blue,
stripped the stems and packed the buds
in a jar with alcohol gurgling deep. We left
the jar for months in our tight pantry,
among artichoke hearts and olives,
keeping it like food.

This winter, amid the buffeting brown and gray,
dulled by the dour churches and salt scud,
wrinkled truck drivers and breath smoked
with cold, I opened the jar, and the smell
spilled out, spicy-thick and vibrant
as the day I picked it, drenched in alcohol
that normally kills, preserving an essence
like light captured in silver, a photograph
of a smell. The foreign musk mingled with steel,
the rot of frost kill, canning steam and the whiff
of stored cabbage, all sharpened by cold.

The Rift

> "if I stepped out of my body I would break
> Into blossom."
> —James Wright, "A Blessing."

Daisies at dusk
nod their blossoms
and drop light into fog
haunting the garden edges—

the drain pipe, the dented fender,
the laconic lid of the garbage can.
The curb crumbles at the drive—
last season's leaves thatch there.

The crenellated dark forgives
the rift between magical and made—
what the blossoms staunchly hold,
their light and musk, their surety—

how they come back holding summers
in a damp bouquet of the mind's lights,
this lavender, peony, lily and cranesbill,
luminous by a shed of ant-pitted wood.

—for Harry Humes

Teleconference with Rain

These voices hover in their own echoes
so I make them real in margin
doodles—lines etching the conversation

plump with details only I can see,
how crows crowd the mountain ash outside—
how words barb themselves in eddies, tail

eating tail as notes spiral and spiral.
I'm in a room with the rest of myself,
tittering into sound far away—

continents away, rain washes over Prague,
Hong Kong, the Bering Strait—the exotic imagined
between papers shuffled here.

Calicarpa, washed out, dull coins
against the inky shadows of hemlock
transparent

as this manuscript illuminated in the banality
of the off-handed doodle, the ruled
scribble of underline beneath *I AM SO BORED*.

How do the notes and paper shuffles echo
in the phone? Like the crows' shouts, the sand shift
of amplified air, the skitter of a chair leg

somewhere distant, a reminder
of how we have all but eliminated distance
except when sound echoes it and, staring out

a window, we feel the fascination of far.

Two-Hour Delay

Another morning given over
to the conspiracies of cold,

its weight, its push back to the bed,
its jacketed preparations,

its granular drifts and glistening husks of wind,
its tree-lashed blasts, its waves

frozen in furls and duned eddies,
its whipcrack reflection of sunlight

like a cruel rebuff of warmth,
its glaze of windows,

its clouded capture of the breath,
its confluence of air and water

and sky and void, its gentle
undoing, its frigid yield.

Killing Bees

Finding carpenter bees in decking,
my neighbor tries to balance
his love of all creatures with the buzzing
destruction of his home. He tells me
he decided to co-exist at first, wondering
just how much damage can bugs really do.
Months later, when he sees inside
the hollowed beams above his porch
and feels the soft push of the wood yield
to a finger poke, he envisions a fall,
the roof crashing around one of his kids.
He runs to Wal Mart, a place he detests,
and fills a green basket with can
after can of killing spray and, that evening
enacts an orgy of chemical death—
clouds of it, a stink like lighter fluid
spiked with lemon. He blinks at the haze,
his hand goes to his mouth, again and again.
His children watch him cough, and they crack
the door. His daughter wants to help.
He yells at her to get back. Startled,
she hits her head as she backs up. His son
starts to whimper. The haze thickens
and catches the hue of sunset.
His wife yells to hurry up
and slams the door. A bee staggers
along the beam. He wants to crush it
with his thumb, his tongue, to taste
it die, to make it pay for every hurt,
to sting back for his eyes, his house,
his place, to protect the eyes he sees now,
wet behind the glass doors, the eyes
that will want to look to him forever.

Starting Seeds

I will set up a table near the window,
run heat tape, fill a mister, lay the rows
of seed flats fluffed with peat, then

mark them with the packets, their panels full
optimists of color, the vegetation plump
with the science of test gardens—

cucumbers thick as movie star limbs,
peas lining casings like regiments of pearls,
a tomato the potent heft of a uterus.

These panels predict a bounty.
But now, there's enough snow to bed the plots,
to moisten and turn them soft,

to lay the summer's dust back down.
This is a job I do despite the fact
that it demands I kill half or more

of what I sow. This is a job
of beating blight, weeding the weak, making
the young endure drought to grow strong.

It is violence and preference up close
in sun by the window, where in the ample light
we know it all. Perhaps I overstate—

but prune, sow, dig, and pluck, break
earth and see how you sweat
with toil, are soiled with intent.

Charlie in His 101st Year

I.
Zinc oxide on the hands he recalls as chalky
resin like a smear of lead, another
failure of color in the coal-blasted rail yard,
the smear on the rails through the steam,
the earthy smell of coal smoke
in his face like a mean wind,
through the train's great iron hisses
and the shivering screams of the rails.

He would wrestle his orders out in Dutch
at the bullied demand of German railmen
who barked at the English of Newcomers,
the lumpy Poles and scrubbed Welsh come
to the Lehigh Valley. Can he remember this
every night, staring into the middle horizon
of his solitude, borne of his longevity,
while the night outside is wet in Queens?

II.
His wife died so long ago the dent in the mattress is gone.
The front room is a table lit with candy,
the brightness of sugar against the peach walls.
His rooms are still and dustless
as air unmoved, more photograph than shelter.

In Fort Dix the rooms were tented canvas,
coarse as his steam hardened skin, their color
a new smear over the short commands.
He taught men to wield rifles
and the ornament of their uniforms,
their faces taut with the shine of plenty,
bellies lean but thick with meat,
arms bulked like trains.
The cabin's dirt lawns were ringed in stone
and yews, tidy and hedged, kept the dust down.

A thousand men in lines comforted him.

III.
In a restaurant, the waiter leans down
to place Charlie's hand close to the fine line
on a credit card slip, so he can sign.

The yews around his house grew well,
and now block his view. A penance
for prudence. Sometimes he wonders
how pleased he might have been to die in a penumbra
of booze, by a fire, among the poplars of Palmerton,
within earshot of the only sounds he still hears from there:
trains shifting rails, a conductor's howl, a mad bell.

IV.
He remembers the soldiers: missing teeth
and blue tattoos, the killers and con men,
scholars and farm boys, all toting smokes
and bibles fit to the palms of their hands.

He grew out of the Great War, made a life in commerce
of dreams, a film man grinning at the advent
of sound. Crowded theatre in Hollywood, he lurked
in the back, felt faces wince at the first sounds
of war on the newsreels. He thought of trains.

In the decades he spent feeling the fading of light,
reels of Victory Gardens and war bonds, the sweet
riveter and the lack of chocolate, he tasted the domestic
suffering of the grandest home gestures. He
was born the year Whitman died

his first breaths of air quickened with the death
of optimism, the death of frontier, the innocent
traveler, and he spent a life chasing that first
taste he never knew. Instead he inhaled the flash
of gun carbon, the coal smoke of locomotives, gasoline
ozone and a whiff of fallout.

V.
He thinks the yew out his window has spirit
moving through cells in a way still unexplained—
the faith in that process the closest he gets to hope,
the last shreds he has of belief in something
beyond his staunch acknowledgement of time,
as he has aged beyond even the last suspicions
of a God.

He thinks he has an idea, now,
of what God could be—
his vision marbles, and he fumbles quickly for his tea,
sips, long since accustomed to burning his tongue.
The taste is metal, sharp, and clear.

4. Brown with Its Own Neverending

Linnaeus Never Said A Peony Was Bashful

but the gardeners of the nineteenth century,
gathered by lichened cherubs and urns,
deigned the peony a bashful bloom,
an icon for the brush strokes
of embarrassed painters.

                  Looking at the flower's
bunched petticoats on a May afternoon,
as it exhales stringent musk and
glaring color, bashful is not the word—
unless you'd seen the bud, tight,
coaxed open by the ministrations
of a hundred ant legs, lulled to
exhibition by small industry, by
those crawling for sugar.

Quartet on Beauty and Mystery

I.

"Last night," you said, "last night I had a dream
I was at the Oscars (*and I saw you besequined and jaunty*
in the Klingon styles of Gaultier, wearing a happy-face pin,
a tin circle of beauty) and you know the curving staircase
they descend? At the base stood Jon-Benet Ramsey
saying to everyone, 'I am pretty, I am pretty' and she
would keep turning and saying 'I am pretty, I am
pretty' and it broke my heart (*and I felt the sundered*
corpuscles, the thrumming of the cardiac muscle like the tremor
in the spasm of an eyelid, the giveaway tremble of our flesh
we can't control)—just broke my heart."
It was the morning bean sprouts broke the soil,
the morning your throat nearly closed from drought,
when milk started to go bad, the bacteria
build-up burgeoning within the white plastic,
a day when it felt as though everything else
should start. It was the morning when the sun
burned on the pollen of the windshield, when spring
seemed nasty, a mean movement of the planet,
and I could think only of the dream you told me.
I am pretty I am pretty. The small parts of me, the worst
parts, wonder if this was a mantra
said prior to the killing.

II.

In our house the ficus tree is dying for spring
to be returned to the yard—and this morning
it senses the proximity of the season: more leaves
drop than is usual (*and I hear the scuttle of leaves*
curled into tubes, dried by a kiln of sunless air, they aerofoil
the wood floors while cold banks the windows in rime
and frost etched glass is brittle against the sky). The gardens
are stick tips snagging leaves and tall windows
give us a golden view of slowness. We wait
for leaves to unfurl. As you dress, it's controlled,

your deliberate presentation, your cultivation of self—
to what degree did she choose her clothes?
How did she understand cultivation? I remember
a title by Baudelaire, *The Flowers of Evil,* and I see
them gnash their petals like teeth at this world. Her teeth
were smaller than pinky nails, soft bone
of a child's skull, and her teeth showed so often
the tempting glimmer of bone that lets us glimpse
the promise of a skull. Outside, soil and worms work
and we gulp peas from the vine snarl, look forward
to the give of squashing tomatoes in molars, the selfish
bite of richness, the contrast of vegetables and fashion, dirt
and now of Jon-Benet's dance, of the lenses
we use to view it: the now of a restaurant,
of evening, when we see two people close
in a restaurant, hear that they are each divorced,
and they are trying hard to enjoy the fatty chimichangas
and seem urbane, cosmopolitan, chi-chi
in a Chi-Chi's. When we saw them you said
"Divorce is for the selfish. Divorced people
do things 'for me.' They are like babies." And I
thought of the baby murdered who preened,
ass in the air for her mother, (*and I smell the hairspray,
the ethanol sting of the nostrils, and the purse smell of makeup
smeared against the pores that barely show, her skin
smooth beyond the need for dark*) who likely did nothing
for herself. Doing things for oneself is the childish
thing few children are aware they do. The awareness
makes it adult. To see her eyes in slow motion dance
reels tells nothing of awareness. See the *nothing
that is not there and the nothing that is.*

III.
There is patience in everything. You once told me
only the incontinent truly learn patience.
You once told me Mozart was the vanilla
of music, (*and I hear the trill and flutter,
arpeggiate and dip in a rococo gilding of noise
so much like a tranquilizer*) so ubiquitous
it is never really flavor. You once told me I

underestimate your capacity for understanding
and you understand so many things: the movement
of protein through electricity, the leavening
of bread, the electromagnetic fields of the continents
that lie beneath the wingspans of birds, (*and I feel*
the polar leaning of bacteria in their nasal cavities,
weighted beaks, the paper clip on a paper
airplane, the dynamics of flight so small here in the hollow
bones of birds) the cold heart of a slab of ice,
a sculpture of steel, you understand blood
movement and pressure, bone harvests
and the topography of the head.
But what you really know exists
in the traceries of neurons left
to their own devices, the moments
of somnolent travel that take you
to the edge of an island in sleep,
where a little girl's statement echoes
over the waves, when beauty
erodes the ugly barbs that stick
to truth. Beauty and truth puts too clean
a face on it—truth is seldom self-evident,
usually more of a mystery. Beauty and
mystery is more to the point.

IV.
All seasons speak of loss in an eloquence
of weather, sun that tumbles by in a drift
moving the sky to a day's end.
The order of *this* day (*the day of articulating*
dreams, of visions mired in tragedy, inspired by TV,
the tabloid news seep into the cortex and behind
the eyes, the order of THIS day) I take as is—
its contemplation of loss and its moments
of beauty wrapped in the early mist
above the furrows of the nursery
where I work. In back fields, trees grow old
in their baskets, their roots vault away
from the ball and plunge into the soil
where once, like a child dipping a toe

in water, the root first touched, sent
warning back along its cells, each new
one pushing out toward water
until, days later, millions of jolts of electricity
later, the root tip has pushed earth
aside, seamless—a product of not moving.
This spring day I try to knock the mulch aside
and it's solid, fastened down in tufts
of roots, the wood and humus a dense thatch,
more settled than dust, the tree's slight lean
now fixed, forever askance. I have to re-dig it,
separate it from the mountain it has made,
from its air, from its space above the surface.
All that is lost in that movement, all the potential
transformed into the actual, begets beauty,
a mystery that says we go on.

Euterpe

Myth-burdened and now strange,
deaf in one ear, your iron lungs
stunned shut, wheezing with hope
and croup. It's old to say you're old,
but there it is: you, living with your cats
in a walk-up dust bowl by a river
brown with its own neverending,
or in a planned community,
your sisters on the other side,
taking stained glass classes once
weekly in the community center.

What have you to talk about
but what is gone only from sight,
what drifts through the reeds
in the treatment basins at town's edge,
what silt measures in storm drains,
what music flows lost in radio hiss?
If you still see your sisters, what do you
chatter back over sly fingers of bourbon,
that amber to chase the meds, give them kick,
while you play spit with the verve of cement?

Or do we have even a busman's idea
what it looks like where you sit?
Morning's crystal tumult emerges not as time
but as sound, a racket bird-thick and steely,
more poetry than we'll ever know, you say—
and then you grumble to your sisters
on the phone or over Grape Nuts
of how we all have forgotten morning
after all these years, as if it's too tired,
as if fascination ages in the face of the repeat,
as if to sing morning once is to get it—
even though thick-fisted notion clutching
has yet to get near it, to rub its briars, flick its buttons.

If they ever did, you spit, it would stifle the sun,
embarrassed as it would be, that some turtleneck
had the *cojones* to write what was *there*,
and doing so, undid it all.

Night Thoughts in Central Pennsylvania

Honeysuckle our jasmine in June—
weighs the gloaming air with scent,
and runs through curtains' eyelet lace
above Ken's century-old boot shop
that opened back when everyone,
everyone went to church, even
as some old women say even
the Jews went to church,
because that was what you did.
Narrow thoughts of the Jesus cult
fill today's opinion page, alongside
the gripes about the school board's
conspiracy of property taxes.
We roll down pickup windows,
smell honeysuckle's clean perfume
as it washes the air and we know
that pestilence of sweet, that binding
beauty and its erosion of height.
We know that full scent.
Bellefonte is fading—
dragging back its past in gaslights
and holiday reenactments,
Victorian house tours and monuments
to this community of fear
perched in the woods.
What they don't rail about in the paper,
what we hardly mention to one another,
is the two Russians, dead on Centre
Hall mountain. They drove too fast.
The police reported a fire
had started from a discarded French
cigarette tossed on the floor.
In the paper, the firefighters
stand tall near the totaled Peugeot.
The reporter made sure
to mention the cigarette,

French, how they were Russian, lived
in assisted housing, as though
we cheer their deaths as some
divine retribution for their cigarettes,
their cavalier driving, the Cyrillic
characters endorsing the welfare check,
the ways we imagine they rejected Christ.
In their picture in the newspaper,
from their passports, they look
older than we will ever be.
In the police log, more.
A man shoots a woman
after tormenting her for years.
He left a severed deer head in her fridge.
He broke in once and smashed
all her light bulbs. He poured gas
and lit it, to burn symbols in her lawn.
His coworkers at the Corning plant
said he seemed a good guy.
He stole her light, he burned
himself into her lawn,
he broke her with torment,
he smashed her head.
We hate how we hope she smelled
this air thickened with musk,
that some sweetness held to her.
Some would hope the same for him.
We are too small to do the same.
Our only hope is what we know
of this scent, its source, this plague
of vine, this beautiful strangler.

Birthplace of Memorial Day

That day, a man drives a parade float
over his mother. Seniors in lawn chairs grumble,

can't see the EMTs, the ambulance, wonder why
the parade has stopped and the baton groups

have stalled the twirling of affected grace. Their mothers
spritz them with water bottles, lipstick

themselves in the reflection of their men's fenders.
Those scant with beards and cigarette eyes

lurk under caps with chainsaw logos and beer brands
in their trucks with roof-mounted woofers

blasting dance mixes of Celine Dion
at their daughters and nieces doing hip grinds

and other moves mimicked from MTV
in home-sewn costumes dense with sequins

hanging on their rod-straight frames. No one knows
the fate of the woman far ahead, or the mind

of the man who hit her, who is gone suddenly,
hunkered under the fire hall barbecue tent,

where the men in trucks normally gather on Thursdays
to complain about their wives or their kids or to wince

at what they don't say about who died or to gripe
about respect, how fires don't douse themselves. But they do,

all the time. They burn and burn and exhaust
their tinder, their air, their abundance, their light.

Gabriel Welsch is a former garden designer and nurseryman. His poems, stories, essays and reviews have appeared in dozens of magazines and journals, including *Mid-American Review, Harvard Review, New Letters, Missouri Review, Spoon River Poetry Review, Crab Orchard Review, Georgia Review, Ascent, Chautauqua Literary Journal,* and *Rapportage.* In 2003, he received a Pennsylvania Arts Council Individual Artist's Fellowship for Fiction, and in 2002 was the inaugural Thoreau Poet in Residence at the Toledo Botanical Garden. He lives in State College, PA, with his wife, Jill, and daughter, Bella, and works at Penn State (where he earned an MFA in 1998) in alumni relations and development for the College of the Liberal Arts.